A Story About Learning Values

by JESSICA L. SIMONS

Mom – We've been through a lot together, and your strength always helps me to persevere. You inspire me daily as my mom and my friend!

Dad, Liz, and CWC – Thanks for your love and endless support. I am who I am because of you!

And for my two special little loves – You and your hugs make my heart full and my world a happier place.

ISBN 978-0-692-99537-2

Library of Congress Control No.: 2017917007

Published by JessCares LLC

Hugs make us feel special
Loved from the start
All comfy and warm
They fill up our heart.

Hugs make us feel happy.
Hugs make us feel glad.
They make us feel better
When we are sad.

If you want the same feeling
A hug can provide
Be helpful and share
To feel good inside.

If you're kind and you're nice
To whomever you meet
If you're thoughtful and good
Respectful and sweet

If you follow the rules
Show good manners too
Cooperate and care
More hugs will find you.

Read along, come with us
and you'll see from the start
Ways you can get HUGS to fill up your heart!

We had to get up
Get ready for school.
Then mom picked the outfits
That just weren't cool.

We cried and we screamed
"This just isn't fair!"
Who gives her the right
To decide what we wear?

The stripes and the dots
Match perfectly well.
My brother's high socks
Also look swell.

But knowing she loves us
We meet her halfway.
The socks and the dots
We ditch for today.

We put on our shoes.
We get in the car.
We show her we care.
To us she's a star.

We learned a great lesson.
Then a hug touched our heart.
To **cooperate** is better.
Now we did our part.

What else can we do?
Turn the page and you'll see
How HUGS can be earned
For you and for me!

We can't wait to eat
Our dinner at night.
We cry and we whine
Till our food's in sight.

We grab and we shove
We eat with our hands.
"Where's my drink? I want more!"
We quickly demand.

But we know it's not nice
To act out this way.
We should wait till they're done
Till we run off to play.

So we sat at the table
We acted polite.
We showed our good manners
At dinner tonight.

We learned a great lesson.
Then a hug touched our heart.
We showed our **good manners**.
Now we did our part.

**What else can we do?
Turn the page and you'll see
How HUGS can be earned
For you and for me!**

We see the bus coming
To take us to school.
We now have a chance
To follow each rule.

Sit down, buckle up
Don’t grab for a seat.
Don’t yell, don’t jump
Don’t kick with your feet.

But it was too hard
To do what we should.
So we misbehaved
And up we stood.

“Sit down!” yelled the driver,
“Sit where you belong!
No pushing or punching!
Don’t do anything wrong!”

BUS
74
STOP

STOP
SCHOOL BUS
74

We listened and did
Whatever we could.
We followed the rules.
We tried to be good.

We learned a great lesson.
Then a hug touched our heart.
We **followed the rules**.
Now we did our part.

What else can we do?
Turn the page and you'll see
How HUGS can be earned
For you and for me!

We heard some sounds.
We then saw the crowd
And a little girl crying
As the noises got loud.

Kids called her some names.
They made her feel bad.
They made fun of her.
She looked really sad.

Was it her shoes?
Was it her dress?
Why did they think
She was such a mess?

No matter the reason
No matter the why
It's just never nice
To make someone cry.

We went over to help
So those kids could see
That they shouldn't be nasty
It's no way to be.

Don't make fun of people.
Don't make them feel sad.
Be kind, be nice.
Make others feel glad.

We learned a great lesson.
Then a hug touched our heart.
To be **thoughtful** is better.
Now we did our part.

**What else can we do?
Turn the page and you'll see
How HUGS can be earned
For you and for me!**

We went to the park.
I climbed on the beam.
"Hold my hand, brother!"
I started to scream.

But he ran away
As I started to fall
To have his own fun
Ignoring my call.

I started to cry
As I fell on the ground.
Tears on my face
Made him turn around.

He quickly came running
To help me to see
That I really could do it.
He believed in me.

Back up I got
His hand holding mine.
He showed me his love.
This time I was fine.

We learned a great lesson.
Then a hug touched our heart.
To be **helpful** is better.
Now we did our part.

What else can we do?
Turn the page and you'll see
How HUGS can be earned
For you and for me!

When school is out
And summer is in
We head to the beach
To play and to swim.

We get there and see
All the fun to be had
The water, the waves.
But the rules could be bad.

Papa says, "Be careful,
You must listen to me.
The day will be great
As we planned it to be."

In all our excitement
We start kicking the sand.
We run to the water
Without Papa's hand.

"Stop, wait for me!"
We hear Papa shout.
We remember the rules
And quickly get out.

We promise to listen.
We'll do as we're told.
So we'll get to come back
Before it gets cold.

We learned a great lesson.
Then a hug touched our heart.
To **respect** is much better.
Now we did our part.

What else can we do?
Turn the page and you'll see
How HUGS can be earned
For you and for me!

The toy in the room
I thought it was mine.
But my sister grabbed first
And started to whine.

She thought it was hers.
She wanted it too.
She held it so tightly
She broke it in two.

It was then that I thought
To give her a turn.
That by doing for others
She'll quickly learn.

That sharing is caring.
That kindness is key.
That playing together
Is more fun, she'll see.

So I fixed up the toy
I did what I could.
When I saw she was happy
I, too, felt good.

Next time she'll know
How to act when we play.
How to be nice and fair
And just what to say.

We learned a great lesson
Then a hug touched our heart
To **share** is much better
Now we did our part.

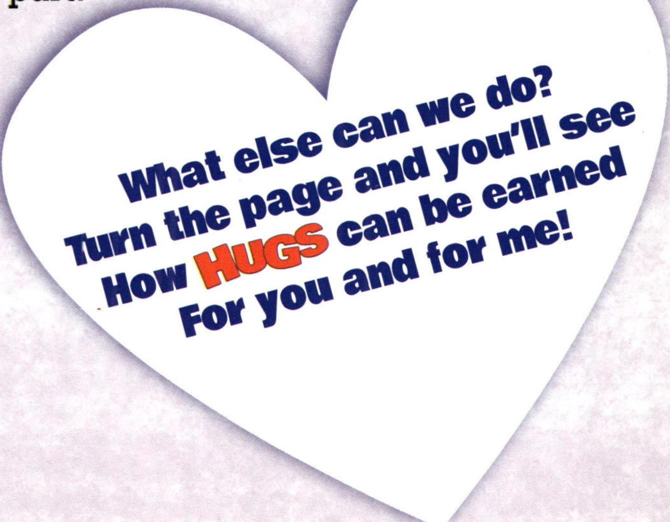

We've shown you a few
Lessons we've learned
But many more hugs
We can still earn.

In whatever we do
For whomever we meet
We'll **share** and we'll care
Be **helpful** and sweet.

We'll **follow the rules**
Show **good manners** too.
Cooperate, be **thoughtful**
Respectful and true.

So starting tomorrow
Wake up, do your part.
For this isn't the end
It's only the start.

Find other ways.
Look and you'll see
There are hugs all around
For you and for me.

The End

...or just the beginning!

So now what should they do?
Go to our website –
www.TheHugsmilers.com
But WHY?
To learn ways to get hugs
But WHY?
To get the same feeling
a hug can provide
They'll learn more ways
To feel good inside.
So what else is on our website?
Lots to know about
our group of "huggers"
Our group of what?
Huggers like us
What does that mean?
Kids who find ways to
give and get hugs
But why would they want to?
'Cause hugs will make them feel happy.
They'll make them feel glad.
Hugs will make them feel better
When they are sad.

So, if you find ways to give and get hugs...
It just might make the world a kinder and happier place!

**What are you waiting for?
GO to our website now, RIGHT NOW!**

www.TheHugsmilers.com

Jessica L. Simons is a hugger at heart – always believing in the power of kindness and happiness and doing all she can to bring that feeling to others. With a Masters in Special Education from Fordham University and a Bachelor of Arts degree in Communications and Studio Art from New York University, Jess is combining her teaching experience and passion for doing good into her first children's book. She is looking to help kids everywhere learn important life lessons, and in a fun way, inspire them to be better people in their homes, in their schools and in their communities. She is married with two young children – her very own "Hugsmilers" - and resides in Westchester, New York. She is known for making the best banana bread, which is another small way that she brings smiles to people's hearts.

**Making the world a better place,
one HUG at a time!**